the p

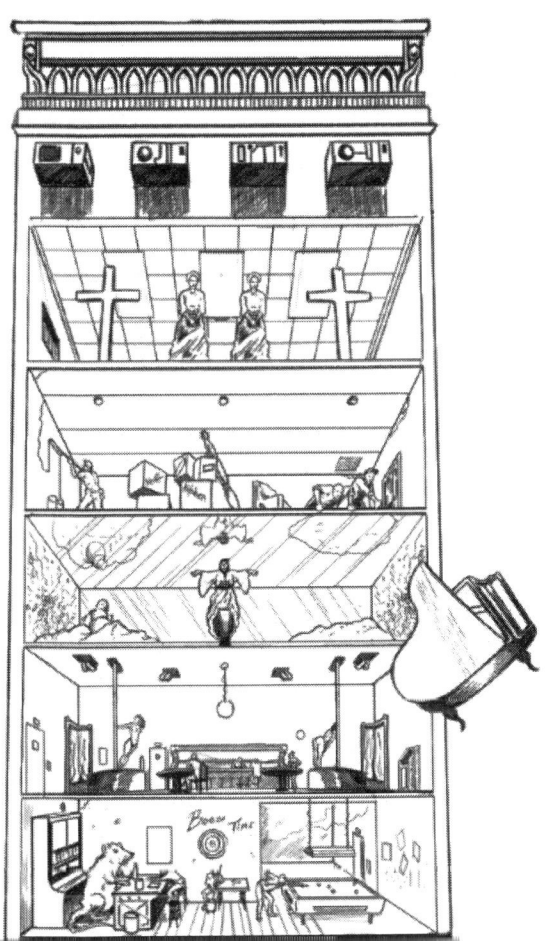

# dave newman

Copyright ©2015 by Dave Newman
All rights reserved.

Published by White Gorilla Press
186 Waterview Avenue
Belford, NJ 07718

www.whitegorillapress.com

Cover and interior design by W. Clay Chastain
www.williamchastain.com
Twitter: @WCChastain

These poems are works of fiction. Any resemblance to actual persons, living or dead, is entirely coincidental.

No part of this book can be reproduced in any medium without the written consent of the publisher.

ISBN: 0-9884459-3-X
ISBN-13: 978-0-9884459-3-2

This book is for Adam Matcho, whose life as a writer, father, and husband consistently inspires my own.

Watch greasing your wheels with that Flood City rum, brother.

These kids today will run you over in the street.

You spend half a life
looking for your own
particular heaven,
expecting to be found
one day on a sidewalk
in a bad neighborhood,
face toward the sky,
hoping some body saw
a blaze of light perhaps
a shooting star
some thing to make it
mean some thing.
Yo, that brilliance there,
is it you?

— *Lucille Clifton*

Get out of this pigsty

—*Nicanor Parra*

# DETROIT, MICHIGAN

"You want smack?" he says. "Downtown."
He loads the boxes. I write the bills.
I've been eating pep-pills like a fiend
but not getting the spunk I need.
The secretary here says she wants a date.
Here's the truth: we all want a date.
A man is coming Thursday to interview me
for a position they're creating in Iowa.
If I keep taking drugs, Detroit isn't so bad.
When I'm sober, I can't stand the water.
The rivers back home aren't clean
but I miss them. Can you imagine Iowa?
Corn and all those flat open spaces
and farm kids cooking crystal meth.
Love is not geography, except when it is.
The smack sells in the ghetto near Tiger Stadium.
The man with the gold tooth knows his Presidents.
He counts the bills. I grind the gears.
After that I sit quietly in some dank bar where
the women are naked except for garters and hairspray.
It's true I write the bills but I also throw the boxes.
My knuckles are bruised, I can see the colors.
If you're from where I'm from, and you do the work
I do, you leave. I shouldn't drink when I do dope.
It's like dreaming of Dee's Bar and the woman
bartender with bleached blonde hair who hates
the jukebox but in a good way. I work so much
I lose whole days. A stripper pushes her huge
breasts together and says "Honey, you look sad."

I miss Pittsburgh like crazy.

# 1

*I hope you're happy believing whatever it is you believe
If you can afford it, please, buy the next round*

## THIS FUCKER SAYS

he's going to throw me in the Allegheny River.

"Why's that?" I say.

"You're looking at me" he says.

It's three a.m. and he's a lot drunk.
        You can hear the water.
        You can hear my lungs.

Sometimes I tell time by reading
the clock on the mountain.

Sometimes I walk so I can sleep.

The drunk pulls a pack of cigarettes
        like a gun
        and asks for a light.

The river beneath us is the Monongahela.

West is Ohio, south is West Virginia
        north is New York, east is the worst.

I know it sounds confusing
but no one is getting tossed in the Allegheny.

Sometimes I get lost in my own neighborhood.

That's why I left my apartment.

That's why I'm going home.

## "BUY ME A DRINK"

she says then slams her purse on the bar.

"Okay" I say and buy her a drink.

The bartender is a mouse
        with a tail of hair
        dangling in his eyes.
He's 24 or 25 and will be embarrassed
by all of this when he sobers up
and goes back to law school.

The woman says "Look in here"
and peers into her purse
        which is empty as her womb.

"Did someone rob you?" I say.

"I forgot to put anything in here" she says.

Some days my life is like that:
        I stay up all night reading
        then walk out without my brain.

"Buy me another drink?" the woman says
        clicking the clasp on her purse
            a little less arrogant
                a little more hopeful.

The mouse scurries over
and takes a couple ones from my pile.

I hope he remembers me
        when we finally go to court.

## CLUB BOOM

A nineteen-year-old woman with a fake ID dances her way from Erie, Pennsylvania—where she lives in a two-room apartment with her boyfriend who delivers pizzas for his uncle—to the all-night bar at Club Boom in Pittsburgh's Strip District.

She's drunk now.

The music is loud.

The flashing lights will make you blind but she thinks she could live here for a couple years: waitress, bartend, or even dance naked.

She won a wet t-shirt contest once and dudes bought her drinks all night.

She kisses a woman in the bathroom and it feels harder than she expected.

The bitches here all have big hair.

Midnight, whiskey sour.

Condoms in her purse.

She thought everyone would be doing coke or ecstasy or something better than the bathtub speed they snort back in Erie but all they do here is slam shots and suck drinks with straws.

She did acid once with her boyfriend when they were still in high school and she got scared and puked pizza through her nose.

She thinks she smells pot but it could be the stink from dancing.

The people in Pittsburgh sweat too much but no one promised they wouldn't.

Part of getting discovered is discovering yourself, she thinks, and drinks an IC Light which tastes as bad as the PBR they serve at the Plaza Lounge back in Erie where the bartender thinks she's 25 years old and gives her free cigarettes and pretzels.

Two guys in tight silk shirts dance with each other and they motion for her to come out and join.

Later, she thinks.

Discovered, discovery.

The bartender has the sexiest salt-and-pepper hair. He walks with a slight limp and the tattoo on his forearm is a smudge of black and green ink.

She's never done it with an older guy.

When he comes back around, she tips him a dollar and asks his name.

It's 1:56 a.m.

His name is Marcus and he wants to go home.

# THE POURER AND THE DRINKS

The rag picks itself up at the end of the night
and runs circles across the tables and booths.
The glasses wash themselves, the floor sweeps up.

The old man, who usually tends bar, sits and drinks.
His name is Harris and he's decided the work
        can do itself, just like people imagine.
It's 2:15 a.m. and the doors are locked, lights down low.

The kid who owns this place wants to shut it down.
Last week he said "I'm just tired of all the bullshit."

The kid who owns the place is 43 years old.
He has three college degrees and never worked.
He comes into the bar every 10 days and implies
the black guy who cooks in the back steals cheese.

The bar used to belong to the kid's dad
who ran things for 39 years until he died
        staring at a donut
        in the Paddy Cake bakery
when a blood clot moved from his leg to his heart.
The kid's dad worked five days a week
and took a one-week vacation once a year
to Ocean City, Maryland to eat blue crabs.
        He drank while he tended
        and was generally loved
        except by those he refused credit
        or clubbed with a broom handle
        he'd broken off and taped-up.
He wanted his kid to get an education.
He wanted his kid to have soft hands.

He wanted his kid to not wake up
with the smell of Miller beer in his nose
and all his shirts, even the laundered ones
    stinking like day-old cigarettes.

Harris knows how disappointed the dad would be.
They were best friends and drinking buddies
    and they were the first men
    at the poker tables
    when the casino opened
    in Pittsburgh.

The kid who owns the bar now does not drink.

The heart is a strange organ.
    You can beat it up
    or love it too much, depending.

Honestly, Harris thinks, the kid owned
too many designer tennis shoes growing up.

The dad smoked two packs of Marlboros a day
since he was 12 years old and worked 13 years
for Westinghouse before they shut the plant down.
The money for the bar came sideways and up alleys.
It started as horse racing and boxing matches
and became something else then came back legit.

The kid who owns the bar can't do payroll
    so Harris barely pays taxes
    and mostly collects under the table
        the same way he started
        when he used to clean up
        the peanut shells

>            the guys from Westinghouse
>            tossed on the floor.

When the son took over the bar, he said
"I want to know everything about this place"
>            so Harris pulled out a mop
>            and the kid said
"I don't need to see that shit."
When Harris tried to show him
the fancy new cash register
>            he said "This is bullshit"
>            and ordered some cheese sticks
>            which Harris dumped in a fryer
>            then blotted with a paper towel.
The son used to play in a hippie rock band
>            but quit because it was bullshit.

Everything, the son believes, is bullshit.

Harris is 77 years old and never worked
another job except for two years in the Army
>            between Korea and Vietnam.
He used to get blowjobs in the backroom
>            by the mop bucket
>            from a beautiful waitress
>            and now he calls his daughter
>            on his cell phone
to let her know he's lived another day.
You work so your kids can work less.
The plan can succeed and still fail.

The bar will shut down or it won't.

The kid gave Harris a frozen turkey last November
then asked if he could work Thanksgiving night.

Harris doesn't have a pension
but he has a little Social Security
and he's saved a lot, neatly
gum-banded 20s stacked in shoeboxes
       in his basement.
       It's all numbered now
              the years and the bottles.
       Harris counts the shots he pours
             each night for each person.

On his 21st birthday, 56 years ago, the owner
       the real owner, the dad
tied a balloon to Harris' back belt loop
and made every customer pay a dollar
       to buy Harris a drink.
       Understand that?
       To buy Harris a drink
       each person had to pay
              Harris
              a dollar.
       Some paid five, some paid 20.
       One guy paid in cigarettes
             and silver change.
Harris went home drunk with 80 bucks
       knowing he'd found a job for life.

Now the floor mops itself and why not.

Maybe the spoiled kid is right: it's all bullshit.

But the spoiled kid is wrong. it's only bullshit
       when bullshit is what you believe.

Harris loves his daughter.

Whatever dreams he dreamed
        were for her
        and so her life
        is his in a way.
She walks into the courthouse
        downtown
        and pops open
        her briefcase
and he could be every legal paper she reads.

Harris' great grandfather
picked cotton in Mississippi
and his grandfather made Fords
        in Michigan
and his dad made steel
in the Carrie Furnaces in Rankin.
To tend bar and go unrecognized
by a spoiled peckerwood is not so bad.

Harris pulls out his cell phone
        and sets it on the table.

His daughter bitches when he smokes
so he lies a little and fans the air
        when she comes for a visit.

It's 2:30 then 3:00 then almost breakfast.

Harris taps each Pall Mall
        before he puts the cigarette
        to his lips
then works at filling his lungs with smoke.

Tonight the ashtray empties itself.

## I WORK NINE DAYS STRAIGHT

doing physical labor
in 90 degree heat in Pittsburgh

then get a day off

then work 11 days straight

then, because my knees
are stiff as old lumber
I jog a couple laps
around Norwin high school

where a bunch of high school kids
       who do not work 11 days straight
       but need an extra body
recruit me into a basketball game.

I hit a couple layups
and miss a three-pointer
but not embarrassingly so
and it feels good to ball
       to jump and land
       for fun, not money

then I get a cramp in my left calf
like god turning a wrench inside my leg
and I can't walk, let alone hoop.

"Time" I say, trying to make a T with my hands
       then rubbing my cramp
       then ducking a pass
       flying towards my head
       then hobbling off the court.

One of the high schoolers says
        "It must suck getting old"

and I say "Yeah"
        though I hadn't considered
        the physical implications of age
                just the various financial humiliations
until he looked down at me like a cripple.

In my car I head for Giant Eagle
to buy a gallon of orange juice
        to get some potassium
        but my calf keeps cramping
        when I step on the gas.

At home I take six aspirin
        and try to sleep
but mostly flop and stretch.

I go back to work with a limp
and my other calf cramps
        probably from overcompensation

and someone says "You are such a pussy"

and someone else says "Lucky
        we're not carrying pianos"

then I get a cramp in my back
and have to lie down in the grass.

Three guys go out of their way
to walk over me, two with a couch
so I drink a Gatorade
and get back to humping furniture

and the guy who called me a pussy
goes down with a chest cramp
        which is not a chest cramp
        but some sort of tear—

he takes off his shirt
and his left chest muscle
is the size of lily pad
and squirming like a frog

and he says "How's it look?"

and I say "Bad"

and the boss, who did 25 years in the Army
        who has gray hair and abs
comes by and says "Anyone want to work tomorrow?"

and a couple guys raise their hands

and I think: definitely not
        then raise my hand

and a guy in a Motley Crue t-shirt says
        "You want to get a drink?"

and I say "Orange juice?"

and he says "Beers"
and gestures like he's drinking his fist

and I say "Too tired"

and he says "It'll wake you up"
which it might

but the sun rises like a sledgehammer
on mornings after overtime and booze.

Can you imagine doing this at 50?
Can you imagine doing this at 65?

## BEER AS RELIGION
*—for Lou Ickes*

There was god and then there was beer.
Say what you will about my religious
leanings but I believe that. A monk once said
"Beauty lies in the hands of the beer holder."
You can have beauty without beer but can you
have beer without beauty? Maybe, but I won't sit
with you at the bar. My friend Lou bartends over
in Lawrenceville at the Brillo Box. I think he's
getting rich. All those one dollar bills stuffed
in a giant fishbowl, saying "Thank you."
I like drunks. They look so religious.
I like Lou when he's drunk. I like god
if there's a god and if he likes to get drunk.
Lou pours stiff drinks to those of us in need.
I hope you're happy believing whatever it is you believe.
If you can afford it, please, buy the next round.

## MY WALLET MOVES LIKE AN ANGEL

From the glovebox of my car
my wallet flies through the driver's side window

shattering the glass
and knocking off the sideview mirror

then jumps in the pocket
of some broke dude stumbling down Carson Street.

Bless us all. Tell the story.

## JAIL TIME

Midnight is fine, even two a.m., but after that
>	things get weird
>	especially if you're spanked
so I finish the late shift at my second job
>	and go straight home
>	and the next day
>	on the early shift
>	of my first job
>	someone says
"Dom stabbed a guy in the head with a fork."

I say "Why would he do that?"

and the guy says "Fucking Dom"
>	and shrugs

not as an indictment of Dom
>	but as an insight
>	into a certain kind of lifestyle
>	that happens after three a.m.
>	in certain places
>	where certain people meet.

I mean to have something to say
>	to all this violence
>	but it's early
>	and I'm mostly happy
my face didn't end up a roast
with a fork wagging from it.

A day later I see Dom
>	who looks rugged
>	even for Dom

        even for a guy
        who collects trouble
        like pocket change

and I say "Why'd you stab a dude in the face?"

and he says "Fuck that dude"

and I say "Where'd you get a fork?"

and he says "In the kitchen"

and I say "Oh" like a kitchen
is a surprising place to find a fork.

Dom stands there, bored.

I know I do illegal things
but the illegal things I do
        should be legal
so I forgive myself
and confuse myself
        simultaneously.

I also leave my keys in my unlocked car
        which everyone who has ridden with me knows

and somehow Dom decides to borrow my car
        without asking or even telling me

only the left taillight is out
so you have to be careful

about not drinking and driving
and the roads you take

none of which Dom is

so the cops pick him up
and he's driveably drunk
so they take him to a holding cell
        then to county

and the next time I see him
he's dressed in an orange jumpsuit
        handcuffed
          with his ankles
            in shackles.

It costs $180 to get my car from the pound.
I'm pissed at Dom. I'm pissed at myself.

I never run from these things
because where do you run
when this is what you do
and this is where you live
and this is who you work with

but I get weary and I get lost
        I get exhausted
        and confused.

A month later Dom gets into a fight
        with his fiancée's brother.
The brother said something
        probably something like
          "Please don't marry my sister"
and Dom hit him with a whiskey bottle.

Dom insists he's going to pay me back

for the tow truck and the impound
but he's in jail for another 90 days.

Someone at work says
"Those guards peek up your ass
when you go to prison, yo"

and someone else says "Of course they do"

but not me, I drive home safely
in my car with one taillight busted
       the other shining bright.

## POLITICS AND THE AMERICAN LANGUAGE

I'm not against guns.

I'm against being shot.

## DUI

The judge takes my license.
The lawyer takes my money.
The nurse took my blood.
The cop pulled me over.
The bartender poured me drinks.
I drank the drinks.
I drank every drink.
I did this to myself.
        This is my fault.

## I SEE A COP

at four a.m. down near Second Street
and no one is around
       and I'm sober as the river
running too, trying to be healthy

and the cop is dressed
       in a belt holding
mace, a club, a gun
ammo, a taser, handcuffs
a radio, and a flashlight.

The jail is near here.

So is the courthouse.

"Morning, officer" I say.

"Morning, citizen" he says
and waves and smiles.

Just kidding—he looks at me
       with bullet eyes
       and I keep on running.

## THREE FLIGHTS UP

The boss of the moving crew
       who has not lifted anything
       who does not lift things
points at a leather couch with sturdy legs
then points to the third floor
of the medical office building
where the couch now belongs.

I spend a long time measuring the couch
and the elevator, the couch and the elevator

then wish I was a bird, a dinosaur bird.

## FRANK O'HARA WORKS HARD BY NOT WORKING

Frank O'Hara carries furniture with great style
        mostly by asking other people
        to carry the furniture for him
then leaning against a wall and looking good
        in khakis and a t-shirt.

The boss sometimes says "Hey Frank
        get the fuck to work"

but Frank does not get to work.

Frank sneaks off to write poems

while the boss quietly weeps
        into his leather gloves.

We think the boss loves Frank O'Hara
and cannot accept that everyone loves Frank O'Hara.

We carry so much furniture just to get
        Frank O'Hara to loves us

but sometime the boss falls down in his sadness
        and Frank O'Hara says
        "Oh Lana Turner we love you get up"

then we love Frank O'Hara even more.

Frank O'Hara is a small skinny man
who smokes cigarettes for breakfast
and drinks glass bottles of Coke for lunch.
He once gave a loading crew this advice:
"If someone's chasing you

        down the street
        with a knife
you just run, you don't turn around
        and shout:
'Give it up! I was a track star for Mineola Prep!' "

One time we thought Frank was going to carry
        a framed picture
               a pen and ink drawing
               of what was either
               a female vampire
               or Dracula as a cat
but instead of picking it up, he pointed and said:
"Is this an Edward Gorey? I love Ed Gorey!"

        Nights
when we are too exhausted to dream
        Frank O'Hara heads off
        to the beach, to bonfires
        and great love affairs
        with beautiful men
        so we sleep restlessly
        jealous and waiting
        for the next great story
               but
        because of darkness
        and dune buggy traffic
        we worry endlessly.

# A MILLION AND ONE

*A million women have said no to me*
                *—Gerald Locklin*

She's a lawyer and I work
as a key-holder at a mall bookstore
and load boxes for a moving company.

   One night we kiss
and the next night I feel her tits
in the parking lot outside a bar

then I am supposed to call
   but I don't

   because, really
what is a lawyer going to do
with me except, maybe, post my bail.

Time goes by. Nothing changes.
   I head to the bar.
She'd been to Happy Hour at Froggy's
and now she's sloshed on a stool at Mr. Toad's.
   All those amphibians.
   I think it's hilarious.
      She doesn't.

"You never called" she says.

"I called" I say
and buy her a drink
even though I only have
money for 10 beers
and a 20 percent tip
   at closing.

She says "You're a lying snake"

and I think about asking her
if that's her closing argument
       but I don't.

I shrug and stumble off
to talk to a waitress who works
at a bar that televises horse races
       for old men to bet on.

       She's beautiful
and I'd gone down on her once
       in the front seat
       of an economy car
       and after that
I'd proposed to her, joking

and she said "I don't think
my boyfriend would appreciate that"

which was pretty funny but another time
       when she came home with me
       she said
"You weren't serious
about marrying me, huh?"

and I said "No, probably not"

and she said "Then I can't sleep with you"

and I said "I understand"

though of course I didn't

so I made a big bowl
of spaghetti with ground beef
and ate it in bed with the TV on.

After that we were friends
and she once told me
I was the only man
        to have ever
        gone down
        on her
in that little red Honda

and I said "Thanks"
because it sounded like a compliment.

    Back to now:
my drunk lawyer finds me and says
"I'm coming home with you"
        which sounds sexy

but when we arrive at my place

she says "You never called"

and I say "Stop it already"

and she says "But it's important"
and sort of frumps down on my bed.

Well, I know I'm not getting laid
and it's too late to make spaghetti
        so I give her
        some boxer shorts
        and a t-shirt

then try to take them back
once she flips the lights off

and she instantly says
"I don't think we should"

and I agree but not really.

I suppose I'm not her type
       or I am her type
      but can't be
because love is almost never classless

and she probably isn't my type either
because I never have any money
       least of all for dates with lawyers

so we snuggle up in my bed
and wait for morning like shipwrecks
who know supplies are on the way.

Before she leaves
she kisses me and says
       "Call me, I'm serious.
       I want to be with you"

and I say I will

then she asks if I slept with
that waitress with the big boobs

and I say "No"

and she says "Hmm."

It's depressing to bring home
    a drunk woman
who asked to come home in a sexy way
    then not get laid
but I do understand
her ill-conceived logic:

she figures she's setting herself apart
from the other women I've slept with
    but by turning me down
she's only lumping herself in
    with the masses.

**MY FACE**

Men who use pick up lines are pathetic.
Worse: the guy who tries to use not
having a pick-up line as a pick-up line.
I'm a beggar. I get down and weep.
The last woman I slept with was a dark cloud.
I got down on my knees. I wept.
If I could change one thing about
my face, it would be my bank account.

## QUEEN OF BEERS

*I've seen a lot of drunks in my day
but I never seen anyone as drunk as you
and still be able to walk. You're fantastic!*
—*John Cassavetes*

Around midnight I started to clean up the mess
but had to stop to count the number of bottles.

I turned to Jen and said
"You drank 11 beers."

She said "Of course I did, Honey"
and lit another cigarette to make her point.

She went to the bar for the next round
       and didn't come back.

When I found her, she was doing Ouzo shots
with a waiter from the Tavern,
       a middle-aged stripper
       from the Philly Corral,
       and a guy who bartends
       a couple nights a week
       at Ligonier Beach.

I did my shot of Ouzo
       hit the jukebox
       played some pool
and waited for Jen to fall down
       but she didn't, ever.

She slurred her words
       danced a little

      showed me her tits
      when I didn't even ask
      and said
"I think they're lopsided"
then pushed her chin to her chest
      for a better view.

I said "Your tits are fine."

She said "But lopsided?"

I said "Maybe a little but it doesn't matter"

and she said "I know."

She went back to the bar and said
      to no one in particular
"Buy me a shot" and someone did.

I like to be drunk. I like it when people are drunk. I'm seldom impressed by the feats of a drunkard but greatness is greatness so I want to acknowledge that I was impressed by Jen's performance. To weigh 130 pounds and to be able to drink that much and still make it to work the next morning is a talent and talent should be nurtured, and while being drunk is not a particularly hard thing to do, being a good drunk, one who can drink and not fall down, is definitely worthy of praise.

Jen, I dub thee Queen of Beers.

Now, everyone, repeat after me.

## HELL IN A HANDBASKET

My belly feels like a fishbowl
filled with beer, how I shift and slosh

and her eyes look like ice cubes
swimming in another mixed drink.

She puts her hand on my shoulder
and leans near my face to laugh.

My tongue feels like carpet.
Her breath smells like ash.
    We kiss anyway.

Outside I ask her where she's going.
    She smiles and shrugs.

The bartender, locking up, says
    "Go home you two."
The bartender has seen this all before.

The streets are empty, the neon gone.
A small trickle of water leaks
from a fire hydrant and rolls downhill.

I say "So…" but stop myself
because I don't want to sound drunk

and she says "You don't need to be charming"

and I say "I wasn't trying to be charming.
    I'm trying not to slur"

and she starts to laugh so hard
she has to reach across her body

and clutch her shoulder
        to keep her tits
        from bouncing away

and I say "Jesus"

        and she says
"Oh god, I'm jiggling like crazy."

I can't remember the last time
I saw a person do something honest.

I reach in my pocket and find my keys.

She says "My boobs are so big" and smiles.

"Yes" I say "I know."

## EMPTY

Mark wants to get drunk
so he goes to Al's Tavern.

There's unemployment
and, after that, savings.

He likes the time off
but he still wishes for his old job.

In 1983 he made sixteen
an hour as a machinist.

That was good money
but there were Japanese cars.

The cars were red and blue
and their doors closed nicely

and they got 30 mpg around town
and Mark tried not to hate Japan

the Japanese people
which was easier than he imagined

because Ronald Reagan was President
and he was a good one to hate.

If you have to vote for an actor
for President, vote for Humphrey Bogart

in *Casablanca*, not Ronald Reagan
playing the fucking Gipper.

The bar is packed.
Two people wear Burger King uniforms.

After the mill shut down
Mark worked at McDonald's for three days

then got fired because he wouldn't mop
up the puke in the bathroom.

He went to school for a year
then quit to paint houses.

During the summer the hair on his legs
gets knotted with drips of paint.

It's winter now. When a woman
asks to buy him a drink he says "Sure."

No one has bought him a drink in five years.
"I'm Elizabeth" she says.

She wants to shoot pool so they do.
She buys the next round and the next.

Mark says "Seriously, let me buy one."
She refuses. It's her boyfriend's credit card.

Ex-boyfriend. She doesn't mention him
at all one way or the other. She hates him.

She's wearing her denim skirt, short
the sexiest thing she owns

which sort of makes her sad.
In high school she did slutty.

In college she did not.
Now, showing a little cleavage feels bold.

Mark says "Do you always
drink like this?"

She says "Yes."
If he wants to fuck

he has to make the move.
Otherwise she goes home.

Her boyfriend, ex, is somewhere
on business. She thinks he's gay.

Not in a mean way but in a factual way.
She knows she can't change him

but she'd like to. She'd like to
change all the gay men, to have that power.

Mark says "I used to work at McDonald's."
He doesn't know why. He's drunk.

"Me too" she says
"I had pimples for three years."

Elizabeth gets him to bum a cigarette
from another guy. She likes his ass

and his back, his neck
the way it's shaved clean and neat.

She likes neat men. Not gay men.
There is a difference.

"Take me home?" she says and smiles.
He goes for his jean jacket.

She wanted him to ask but so what.
He's hard in her hand.

The bedroom light is dim.
She has to pee but it can wait.

Then it can't.
"One second" she says.

It takes more than a second.
When she comes back, he can't get hard.

She blows him for a minute
and it's like sucking a gummy worm.

He takes her head and says
"Maybe we could sleep for a little bit."

She says "I have to be up for work."
He says "On Saturday?" He says "Oh."

She doesn't have to be at work.
She needs to be alone to make herself better.

The rest can be forgiven.
If she didn't have to pee

he would have stayed hard
and she could have climbed on him

or he could have climbed on her
and there would have been something there

after so many months of being empty.

## EAST PITTSBURGH

Bob Pajich drinking vodka
from a Grimace glass
McDonald's gave away
in 1979 with the purchase
      of a Happy Meal.

# I NEED A PILL

The student loan lady
says "You're not understanding
that I don't care"

and I say
"I do understand that"

then reiterate
that I make minimum wage

and she says
"Pay your bill"

and I stand
in front of
my kitchen
cabinets

total inventory:

2 boxes
of Kraft
Macaroni
& Cheese.

# ROB

## I

Tuesdays, he drinks with Leroy
who works at the Pep Boys in Monroeville
        and never gets a weekend off.

Leroy doesn't ask
where Rob gets his money
and Rob doesn't offer.

Rob studied to be an architect
but quit when he fell in love
        with his professor
        a hot middle-aged woman
        named Rosamond.

Rob turned thirty mid-semester
and all the students were twenty.
        It was stupid.

Rosamond has gigantic tits
and is an avid jogger
so her back often aches
and Rob likes to knead
the muscles going up her spine.
        The muscles around her neck
        put her to sleep
        and she says she has
        the best dreams
        when he works her
                that way.

Rosamond pays the bills and never complains
 even though Rob upgraded her cable
and runs the air-conditioning
from May until mid-September.

Before bed every night
 Rob asks "Do you want me
 to kiss your pussy for a little bit?"

and Rosamond says "That's so sweet."

## II

Thursdays, Rob starts drinking
 with his old friend Dave.

 Dave
running, breathless, sliding in dress shoes
says "I thought you were supposed to be
 some kind of hippie"

and Rob, not breathless, making turns
says "I am some kind of hippie"

as they race from the Sportsman Lounge
 a little before noon, both drunk

seconds after Rob punched the bartender
who said "Now we're supposed to be a nigger bar"

after a black guy bought a six-pack of Stroh's.

Rob hates that shit, the way it's so casual
 how two of his uncles worked
 at the steel mill in Braddock

       and they'd get drunk
       and make nigger jokes
       at Christmas and Easter
       eating fried chicken
with big toothy grins
       sometimes bringing
       malt liquor
       just so they could say
       "Nigger toast"
       and clink quarts.

"Fuck that bartender" Rob says
       inside Dave's car
       and he means
       his uncles too
       as Dave cranks the engine
and lights a cigarette to breathe.

## III

The doctor says "The cast will be off in six weeks."

Rob flexes his fingers outside the cast
and feels embarrassed by everything
       the punch
       the racism
       telling the doctor
       he fell down the stairs.

The emergency room is empty
       except for an old lady
       in a shawl
       sipping coffee
       and waiting
       for her grandson
       to get stitches.

She says "He wrecked his motorcycle"

and Rob says "That's tough."

She says "And you took a nasty spill too"

and Rob holds up his cast
and says "A little bit"
> and means a lot
> means more than
> he can afford.

He doesn't have insurance
and he doesn't know
if Rosamond knows
he doesn't have insurance
> though of course she knows.

## IV

In the hospital parking lot
Dave says "People get what they deserve."

Rob says "Yeah"
> and pretends to be sure.

## V

The next day Rob signs up for medical relief
> and agrees to pay $50 a month
> on an $8000 hospital bill.

Rosamond says "I'm glad you're okay."

Rob says "I'm so lucky you love me."

**VI**

      For six weeks
Rob rubs Rosamond's back with his one good hand.

      For the next six weeks
      while he goes to rehab
he rubs Rosamond's back with his one good hand
      and his right elbow.

**VII**

Rosamond doesn't like Leroy
because he never cleans
the grease from under his nails
and he calls women bitches

but she likes Dave
because Dave has a good job.

Rob doesn't have a job.

Rob quit looking for work
after he met Rosamond.

**VIII**

During the summer Rob feeds the birds.

Rosamond says "Once you start
    you can't stop or they die."

Rob says "I believe that."

## IX

In September Rosamond teaches
an undergraduate class on Frank Lloyd Wright.

Rob drives her to Falling Water
so she can take pictures
and maybe plan a field trip
but they end up making love in the woods.

The rocks and sticks scrape Rob's knees
and Rosamond gets six mosquito bites
              on her ass cheeks.

They shower under a waterfall and laugh.

## X

Leroy gets promoted and starts working
Monday through Friday, 9-5

so Rob quits drinking Tuesdays.

Rosamond loves this.

No more talking about bitches.

## XI

Thursdays are special.

Rosamond teaches her night class
then stays late to correct papers
so she won't have to take anything home

and Rob and Dave share pitchers of Bud
        trying out different bars each week.
This night they talk a lot about Doc Ellis
who claims to have pitched a no-hitter
          after taking a hit of acid.

Dave recently divorced his wife
and feels restless and insecure about being single.

Rob says "You're a good looking guy."

Dave says "I'm trying."

Days, he travels from McDonald's to McDonald's
       servicing their soda machines
but nights he jogs laps around the CMU track
and does three sets of 50 sit-ups on the football field.
       When he gets drunk he talks a lot
       about getting a harder dick
       and flatter stomach
       for these younger ladies.

Rob doesn't know any younger ladies.

He doesn't know anyone
he doesn't want to know anymore.

## XII

Rob and Dave hit a lot of bars
      and talk a lot of baseball.

         One night
high on coke and drinking in a dive bar
      in a black neighborhood

        Rob punches a black dude
        in the face.

They were talking about Dave Parker
        former right fielder
        for the Pirates
        and the time a fan
        threw a battery
        at his head

and suddenly the black dude
        shoved Rob
        and said
"You white motherfuckers hated Dave Parker"

        and Rob
who loved Dave Parker
said "I loved that guy"

and the black dude said
        "Bullshit"
and shoved Rob in the chest

and Rob cracked him in the eye
        with a stiff right.

The black guy fell and stood
and said "Lucky punch, Gary Carter"
and wobbled out the door.

Now Rob looks at the door
        wondering
        if he needs to escape.

Nobody in the bar says anything

        even though they're all black
        and Rob is white
        and Dave is so white
        he looks albino.

The bartender
wrinkled as a crumpled dollar bill
        says "You drink shots?"
and brings the bottle to the bar and leaves it.

Someone else puts a five in the jukebox
and says "You white boys play whatever you want."

They drink until closing, Dave scared
        and Rob feeling like Rob.

At two a.m. the bartender
locks the doors
and no one moves.

He pats Rob on the back
and says "You ever boxed?"

and Rob says "I never boxed."

The bartender says
"You shoulda boxed" and laughs

and another guy says
"White people need good boxers."

## XIII

A year later Rob has a heart attack
while drinking at Mr. Toad's
        on a Thursday afternoon.

The ambulance comes
but his heart won't revive
      a leaky valve
      he was born with.

Dave shows up with his new girlfriend
      a 22-year-old brunette
      with a curvy ass and a tiny waist
      and weeps inside the bar
      then out in the parking lot
      then face-down
      across the street
      on the courthouse lawn.

A cop shows up and says
"I went to high school with that guy.
      Everybody loved him."

## XIV

They have Rob's funeral down in Wilmerding
      at Alfieri's Funeral Home
      because Rob never went
            to church.

Leroy shows up drunk
with greasy nails and asks to speak.

Rosamond can't say no

      and Leroy
reading from something he wrote out
      on a lined sheet
      of yellow paper
      says "Rob was the best.

>He didn't care
>if you were a mechanic
>or a millionaire.
>He treated people, all people—
>>all of us, right?
>>everyone
>>in this
>>fucking room—
>>with respect."

The entire room bawls.

Afterwards, they all get drunk.

## XV

Rosamond thinks she'll never fall in love again
but six months later she starts dating a student
     a young guy who makes good grades
     who comes from money
          nothing at all like Rob.

Six more months and she asks him
not to come around.

Her best friend asks what happened

and Rosamond says "Nothing."

She says "He just wasn't Rob."

# 2

*Poetry readings have very little to do with poetry
just like church has very little to do with god*

# RENNY'S FAMOUS CAR WASH

It's almost Christmas and he's 66 years old. Minimum wage hurts. All he wants to do is buy a laptop computer and put it in the U.S. Mail.

He sweats and the sweat freezes.

His knuckles ache.

Bending is impossible.

The settlement for his back was dwindling so he sold the house.

He has one son, living in Delaware.

The son doesn't call.

Maybe the son would write on a laptop but maybe not.

The boss here, a Chinese woman with a hearing aid and thick glasses, speaks with her hands and expects him to understand.

Dinner is a 99-cent double cheeseburger from McDonald's.

There was a Christmas, 60 years ago, back in West Virginia. His dad was drunk, but drunk-happy. It was evening. They knew about presents but barely. His dad pulled out a .22 rifle, still in the box. "That ain't from Santa Claus," he said. "That's from me and your mom." God, the hills around Beckley. Wild squirrel and deer. Rabbit. He ate possum once because he was starved. His dad got sober and went back to the mine. Sixty years ago. It wasn't a house, it was a cabin. The cold was the coldest he's ever felt and the hunger came on and stayed and the oatmeal tasted like paste but there was this idea of love and his father handing him a gun that he couldn't have possibly afforded.

Nobody at the car wash is named Renny.

Nobody here is famous either.

The job goes through February but he's not sticking around. The vacuum cleaner rattles his ears so that he can barely hear the TV at night.

One room above the Irwin Hotel is better than sleeping in your car. Instant coffee at least smells like coffee. The guy in the next room has a cough like a blast going off in the shaft.

Jesus, all these years. The army was bad but it kept him straight. You do right by people, people do right by you, except when they don't. He never had a wife and the fact is he doesn't know if he's really this boy's father but he raised him the best he could and, come January, he hopes the kid finds time to write a little letter.

# I WRITE AN ARTICLE

and submit it to the local paper

and the editor says "We love it"
and accepts the article

    then says
they'll be paying me $50

so I start adding up the hours spent
traveling, interviewing, writing
    and $50
is way less than minimum wage

which would make a pretty good article
    for a newspaper

but newspapers are not in the habit
of treating themselves like corrupt politicians

and, besides, they never pay me my $50.

They send me a $25 gift certificate
    to a restaurant
        that serves $12 glasses of wine.

## I DON'T DRINK $12 GLASSES OF WINE

Even if I had the money to drink
        a $12 glass of wine
I wouldn't drink a $12 glass of wine.

I might drink two $6 glasses of wine
        depending on the bar
but I'd probably just order a beer.

## AGENTS

This one is not interested in my story collection because stories don't sell. This one likes my novel but not enough to get behind it. Another one is representing *The 300 Pound Tomato*. It's a big book and it takes a lot of time. It's a big tomato and it takes a lot of agents. A lot of agents take a lot of time with publishers talking about big tomatoes and what could be the next big tomato book.

I should plant a garden. I should command the sun. I should move to Italy and crush grapes. Everyone loves books about Italy as long as they're not written by Italians.

But I dislike wine. I like beer. I should drink a lot. I should drink a lot and die. People love books written from the perspective of a dead person.

I love drinking and I'm not against dying and I love money but not gardens and I love books but not the ones published by Random House.

I'm sorry. I'm sorry about my garden. I'm sorry I died. I should have grown a cucumber so large and brilliant it would have saved literature in America.

## I LISTEN TO A POET LECTURE ON THE MUSICALITY OF LANGUAGE, IN PITTSBURGH, DURING THE GREATEST RECESSION IN 100 YEARS

If you call a bag of puke a banana
it's still a bag of puke.

If you puke on the page and send it out
someone will publish your banana.

None of your horrors are so great.
There are words that fit everything.

The Surrealists, at least, had the decency
to call themselves surrealists.

# I KNEW A WOMAN IN GRAD SCHOOL

who said "He wants me to shave it."

He: her boyfriend.

It: her pussy.

I said "That's interesting."

She said "It's creepy.
He wants me to look like a little girl."

I said "Maybe."

But: probably not.

A shaved pussy is a beautiful thing
and I always hated coughing up
furballs during the afterglow anyway.

She said "It's just so fucking perverted."

"Hmm" I said "maybe."

But let's face it:
it's all perverted.

Or: none of it is perverted
when you're doing it
with the right person.

The guy who likes a big bush
may be the same guy

who thinks eating pussy
is for sissies

then fantasizes about humping
his Uncle Murray's toupee.

## HELLO PIANO

Hello Piano, I'm sorry you weigh 800 pounds.
I'm sorry your legs are skinny as a wimp.
I'm sorry there's nowhere to grab, Piano.
I lift weights and jog and you are so fat.
I'd fight you drunk in a bar, Piano.
I'd be like "D'fuck are you looking at?"
But you are owned by a 16-year-old girl
who loves Elton John and Billy Joel
and whose Grandma loves Beethoven
and whose father built this house
with a music room and sound curtains
and who built the next house, a mansion
with a larger music room with thicker
sound curtains and a lower ceiling
and who must surely have $20 bills
like seeds in his pocket he'd like to plant
in the working-class garden of my life.

You and I are the same, Piano.

We're both about to get broken.

We're both about to get played.

## THE COPS SHOW UP

in riot gear with automatic weapons
and spike the boss of the moving crew
to the ground like he's a football.
The air leaves the boss' lungs
like a small tornado blowing
across an open Pennsylvania field
and he squirms and sucks for air
while the cops handcuff his wrists.
This either has something to do
with drugs or the boss' wife
or some misunderstanding
from a previous life or perhaps
the cops have the wrong guy.
The boss can finally breathe
but the cops still maniacally shout
so the rest of us move to the truck
until another bigger boss shows up
to send us home without getting paid.
I drive to my apartment and skip dinner.
I think about cops, I think about bosses.
That night I open one of my favorite novels
and read this line: "Last night
Boris discovered that he was lousy."
The cops are Boris. The bosses are Boris.
I'm Boris. You're Boris too, admit it.

## SCORING DRUGS, TATTOO PARLOR, WESTERN PENNSYLVANIA

Two women, one substantially older
        lounge on stools
        at Spanky's Bar
        in North Versailles.
The older woman is hammered
        the other is jealous.

They are talking about drugs
        and where to buy them.

It's Saturday afternoon
        morning really
        sunny outside
        Route 30 empty
        people still sleeping
in the motel behind this place.

I worked 11 p.m. to 10 a.m.
        and now I am here
        at Spanky's Bar

and the bartender says
        "Shit, I think I just got my period"
and asks if anyone has tampons.

The hammered woman says
"I ain't had a period in years"

and the jealous woman says
"I'll go get you some"

and before I can speak

the bartender says
"I know you're fucking useless"

and everyone laughs.

The bartender buys us all
   two beers
and leaves for Rite Aid.

The woman who is hammered says
   "You get high?"

I say "Sometimes"
and think, for a second
she is going to lay some
powerful new drug on me

   but she says
"You should buy from Kevin.
   Kevin is a cool dude"
   then gives me directions
   to Kevin's tattoo parlor

and the bartender comes back
   with a bag from Rite Aid
   and disappears
   into the ladies room.

Nothing else happens
but we keep drinking
and more people show up

and eventually I think
something should happen

so I drive to the tattoo parlor
  and Kevin has eyes tattooed
  on his eyelids
and he's pretty hammered
  on dope
   like the hammered woman
   at the bar was on dope

and I'm drunk, drunk enough
to think I can buy coke
  from a dope dealer
  who stares at you
  with his eyes closed.

Kevin shows me some photos, some books
  and I'm thinking about
  getting inked again
  because why not
   but not really

and finally he understands
that I'm here for the drugs.

He sits back and says
"I will change your life, dude"
  in a creepy voice
  that's supposed
  to sound important
  then he goes on the nod

and I stand there, drinking
a bottle of beer from a six-pack
I bought at the Grapeville Café.

Kevin snorts from his nose
like he's drowning in heroin
        but doesn't wake up.

I pull up a chair.

Sometimes you go to completion
        even if completion is failure
just to say you finished.

Kevin wakes up and says
"What's on your mind, dude?"

        and I say, joking
"Just thinking about changing my life."

Kevin says "Yeah?"
like he hasn't already suggested it
        and palms his own face
then says "Wait right here, dude"
and moves like's he auditioning
        for a zombie movie.

        I move
like I've been drinking
beer for six hours
and would like to move
like a brain on fire.

Sigmund Freud loved cocaine
and Paul Erdos loved cocaine
and while I'm not going to change
psychology and/or mathematics
I deserve their energy
        and the sharpness
                to think my thoughts.

75

Or I should probably call for help

but how

and I am alone in this room.

Then I am not alone in this room.

Then this room is very crowded

and it's hard to know anyone
when he has Jesus on the cross
        inked across his back.

A woman has a rose tattooed
on her tit and her tit is out.

Another man, another tattoo.

Another woman, another tattoo.

A teardrop underneath your eye
means you've killed someone
unless it means you're crying.

I don't know what's real
or what's for decoration
        and I'm almost
        out of fucking beer.

Kevin, the man with eyes tattooed
on his eyelids, has a snake tattooed
        on his neck.

He's carrying a purse but he won't unzip it.

He asks me for my money, but for what?

He's done something to take him
      off the nod
so the eyes on his eyelids
      stretch open
like snapped window shades

and now my beer is gone.

The room glows with bad energy
when only a couple hours ago
I was in a bar that advertises itself
      as the *O'tay* place to be.

Kevin says "You in?"

I think I am ready to die
      then suddenly know I'm not.

## ON SUICIDE BY HANGING

I'd rather
my heart
not stop
from
the weight
of my ass.

## I FIND A NEW JOB

then find another apartment
the size of a double booth
      in a diner

and put in my two-week notice
at my current job
      delivering industrial parts

then contact my current landlord
who wants a note from my new employer
      so I can break my lease

and my new employer says
      "That's weird"

and I say "What's weird?"

and he says "The note, the lease—
it's all sort of seedy"

and I say "Oh"
and feel sort of seedy and weird.

He looks at me like a smudge on his tie
      he wants to wipe away with his thumb.

My new job involves selling furniture
      which is not exactly grunt work
and my new boss has asked four or five times
      in four or five different ways
      "So why were you working at a job
            delivering industrial parts?"

to which I keep answering
"I was hired as a manager
but everyone has to start
by delivering parts—
it's company policy.
    Even the big bosses started
       by delivering industrial parts"
which is not true, which is a total lie.

I took a job delivering industrial parts
because I saw a sign outside a warehouse
       that said:

    DRIVER NEEDED

and I needed a permanent job
   so I applied.

Are there people who take jobs
for reasons other than desperation?
Is there another way to live and how?
Canned tuna is fucking expensive.
I like hot water and a comfy bed
and a roof during all four seasons.

At the warehouse a guy in green overalls said
      "Why you wanna work here
      if you got a college degree?"

and I said "I love driving"

and he said "You paid for college
to drive a pick-up truck?"

and I said "I didn't pay for college.
    I attended on scholarship"
which was not true, which was a total lie

then the guy at the warehouse
told me what the job paid.

I was completely insulted
    and nodded happily
    and said "Sounds good."

Anyway, my new employer
writes a note on company stationary

and I deliver the note to my current landlord

    and he says
    "It don't mean you get
    your security deposit back"

and I say "It does"

and he says "Why's that?"

and I say "Because my brother is a lawyer
and I'd hate to sue your ass over $300"

and my landlord says "Shit"

and I say "Exactly"

and of course my brother is not a lawyer.
    My brother is an office jockey
    buried in student loans
    and credit card debt.

I have to tell you: all these untruths
really bring me the fuck down.

Steinbeck said, about Americans
       "The poor see themselves
       not as an exploited proletariat
       but as temporarily embarrassed
              millionaires."

Steinbeck, you knew poor people and it made you rich.
I'm angry you are greater than me, you humble fucking genius.

## MORE AMERICAN BULLSHIT

When I take my right bootstrap in my right hand
and my left bootstrap in my left hand
    and try to pull myself up
        I stumble forward and almost fall.

When I try it again and simultaneously
        jump and pull
I get like six inches off the ground.

## THE WORLD'S WORST JOINT ROLLER RESPONDS TO CRITICISM

He says "Your joint looks
like it has a birth defect."

I say "That's not nice."

## EVERYONE IS BROKE AND HORNY

I'm eating her pussy in an alley
        with her skirt up
        and her panties down
        and my tongue on her clit
        though sometimes
        up inside her
        which is not easy to do
considering the angles and the alley

and it's a lot of fun, seriously
        a really great time

but I'm in shorts, on concrete
and there are these little pebbles
grinding into my knees

and I wish I had a better apartment
        one with a landlord
        who does not spy
        on every person
        I bring home.

I wish she wasn't 43 and living with her mom.

**A 17-YEAR-OLD WAITRESS THINKS ABOUT THE OLD GUY AT TABLE NINE WHO WEARS HIS NAPKIN TUCKED BETWEEN HIS SHIRT AND HIS CHINS AND, MINUTES AGO, ASKED HER IF HE COULD BUY HER A DRINK, LATER, IN HIS ROOM**

No wonder
the soup
here
tastes
like spit.

## SHE GETS A JOB WAITRESSING

She takes a waitressing job when she's 17
and makes out with the bartender who is 21
who says he'll go to her Prom then backs out.
She graduates from high school and gets a summer job
at Kennywood, running the Thunderbolt and sort of falls
in love with Keith, who is 29 and services the rides.
Keith has greasy hands and brings her free lemonades
then lets her come back to his apartment to drink beer
as long as she doesn't bring any of her creepy friends.
One night during sex Keith leaves a beautiful grease smudge
on her nipple but in September she leaves for college
and forgets Keith, pretty much, except when she masturbates.
On campus she gets a job in the coffee shop which is boring
and pays shit so she gets a second job as a waitress
at a dumpy Italian place which serves the best pizza rolls
and she falls in love with a cook then the bartender
then another waitress who is 35 with a sunflower tattoo
on her tit that peeks out of her uniform.
Kissing a woman is not as sexy as she'd hoped.
She goes back to dating the bartender who describes
himself as a functional alcoholic which is pretty much true.
He's a good kisser and a decent fuck when he's not unconscious.
She does something like this for the rest of college.
She does something like this after college when she can't find
a real job until she doesn't know what a real job is or care.
Then she gets a real job. No one drinks or kisses or anything.
She gets married and works at loving her husband
who works as a an engineer and cuts the lawn at angles.
She has two kids two years apart who are everything—
sound and light, hearts walking outside her body.
They grow up, they go to college, they find real jobs.
She starts waitressing again when she's 47 and makes out

with a bartender who is 29. She does this for years
until her husband finds out then she stops.
    Then she does this for years:
waitressing, bartenders, slow kissing, sometimes fast.

## FOR FRANK, WHO LOVES PASTA, THE GODFATHER, AND THINKS HIS GRANDMOTHER MAY HAVE BEEN FROM SICILY

Maybe visit Italy
before you get
the map of Italy

tattooed

on your back.

## ALIENS

She was naked, standing on my bed.
With her arms extended she could
almost touch the ceiling.
The ceiling was water-damaged.
"I feel like an alien" she said
and proceeded to jump on the mattress
like it was a trampoline. I was cutting
an apple into small thin moons.
My bathrobe wouldn't stay tied.
She said "I'm flying! I'm flying!"
then my upstairs neighbor pounded
the floor with a broomstick
and I yelled "Sorry!" and finished
with the apple. It was Thursday.
The man with the broomstick
was losing his wife to a man
who did not drive a 1993 Ford Escort.
"That guy can eat me" she said.
"Me too" I said and handed
her the apples which were a little
brown but probably still okay.

## TO THE WOMAN IN THE GROCERY LINE WHO COMPLAINS ABOUT THE MAN IN FRONT OF US BECAUSE HE WEARS NIKE SHOES AND PAYS FOR HIS GROCERIES WITH FOODSTAMPS

It's possible that he
      like many
      intelligent consumers
bought the shoes on sale.

# THE SHORT-CIRCUIT POETRY AUDIENCE

*A good answer to a poem is just to whistle.*
*You know, in Nigeria if someone reads a good*
*poem, the audience doesn't say anything, or clap,*
*they hold their hands out to the sides of their*
*head, like this, open with palms towards the poet,*
*and then wiggle the hands.*
                                              —Robert Bly

I agreed to a reading I really didn't want to read at so I invited Denny's Bar. I invited Todd the cop and his girlfriend the mouse and Christy who was a sales rep for Captain Morgan Spiced Rum and some dude named JoJo Crash and Shelly who skipped her shift waiting tables at HoJo's and 30 other regulars who hadn't read a poem since high school and were, at that time, not making plans to read a poem ever again.

So a slew of drunks squeezed in between the undergraduates with their notebooks and the old folks who still dreamed someone would step up and read a sonnet or some blank verse. The waitress suddenly carried trays full of drinks, instead of plates of calamari.

Poetry readings have very little to do with poetry, just like church has very little to do with god, but I'm as stupid as the next poet and as soon as I took the mic I started to introduce a poem about a job I had cleaning bathrooms like it was a poem of great socio-economic importance and someone yelled "Come on, you were a fucking janitor!" which was the truest thing anyone had ever shouted about my life so I mostly stuck to funny poems that referenced getting jizz in your ear or pissing on a friend's blue car and avoided anything that referenced trees or the moon and later my friend Frankie sang John Denver's "Rocky Mountain High" until I gave up the microphone to head back to Denny's Bar to get drunk and not be around grown men who think blazers are literary.

I understand that Nigeria is supposed to be greater than America by simply being Nigeria so the American poet who dreams a fantastical audience is not responsible for his poems because he is doomed to an audience of illiterate Americans. The thing I find most interesting about Robert Bly is not that I dislike his poems, which I do, but that I disagree with everything he has to say about poetry and by poetry I mean the world.

I'll be reading at East End Book Exchange in Bloomfield or Modern Formations over in Garfield pretty soon so if you're interested, come out. If you're not interested, stay home. Should you wiggle a finger in my direction I'll give you a buck. Stick out your hand and I'll arrange a canned food drive.

## ROBERT BLY

Robert Bly is on stage.
He's reading his poems.
The poems are about

manliness. He's strumming
a little instrument. It looks
like a toy ukulele. His hair

is styled like my granny's.
He's wearing a sweater vest.
I'm embarrassed.

I'm embarrassed for myself.
I'm embarrassed for Robert Bly.
I'm embarrassed for men everywhere.

Take off the sweater vest, Bob.
Break the ukulele. Smash it right
over your own manly head.

## SPIRITUALITY

It's like the guy
who keeps bragging
about being crazy
then flexing
his eyeballs
so they bug out.

He's not crazy.

He's not even fun.

## HELLO, MENNONITES

Once a week the Mennonites from the church up the road show up to tell me that the world is in a bad way.

The Mennonite women wear dresses cut from patterns then sewn with their own thread and their husbands build furniture with old-timey tools.

The women's dresses are not very appealing and their husbands' furniture is overpriced.

Generally, I define rudeness as a stranger knocking on your front door to explain how changing to be more like the stranger will benefit both you and the world.

Nonetheless, I answer.

Nonetheless, I wear boxer shorts.

Nonetheless, I listen and smile.

The world is always in a bad way except when it's in a good way and sometimes the bad way makes possible the good way and vice versa and, anyway, I've been happy lately. My closet is filled with clean shirts and my refrigerator is packed with Coors Light. I sleep where I write. I read in the kitchen. Even though I have bills that will never be paid, I have money in the bank.

Today's traveling Mennonite woman says "Would you want to bring a child into this world?"

I say "Sure!"

She says "What?"

I say "Absolutely."

Her little boy, dressed in a black suit and hiding behind her skirt like a tent, leans out and smiles.

The next week, when I open the door, I say "Good morning, Mennonites."

The following week I say "Beautiful day, Mennonites."

They keep coming back and I keep opening the door.

When I was a kid we went to a non-denominational church that called itself holy and the preacher, sweating and frenzied, stood behind the pulpit and said "Repent! Or ye will burn in the firey pits of Hell."

He actually said that: ye.

The Mennonites never promise damnation but one woman muttered something about "our highly militarized world" while reading from a pamphlet she then handed to me.

I don't know anything about god anymore and I've quit trying to learn how.

I guess it's okay to be religious if you don't kill anyone and the Mennonites, unlike every other fucking religion in the world have that going on, but I ask you, all of you, believers and nonbelievers alike:

What is more simple than three rooms, clean clothes, and a refrigerator filled with bottled booze?

## THE LITTLE WOMAN IN THE PLANE TAKES FLIGHT

After sex, still in bed, laughing, she says
    "My clit is like an aeroplane"
and rubs her finger really fast across her pussy
and makes a vroom-vroom noise with her lips.

## MENNONITES, CLITORIS, BEER

Honestly,
I just liked
the title.

That's it.

**WE'D FOOLED AROUND ONCE AND I LIKED HER AND I THOUGHT SHE LIKED ME BUT MAYBE SHE WAS JUST DRUNK, WHICH IS FINE, I WAS DRUNK TOO, AND I FINALLY GET UP THE COURAGE TO STOP IN THE BAR SHE WORKS AT TO HAVE A BEER AND SHE'S PRETTY DRUNK AND LEADS ME TO AN ALLEY AWAY FROM ALL THE CUSTOMERS AND HANDS ME A HALF-SMOKED JOINT AND KISSES ME**

She says "I'll blow you in the cooler
once I finish my shift"

and I say "Thank you."

## NO THANK YOU

She says "I'll suck your dick"

and I say "No thanks"

and I see her a week later
    at the store
    where she sells
    electronics
    and
even though she's dressed
in a blue polo shirt
and wearing a nametag
and her boss is 10 feet away
    she whispers in my ear
        "I'll suck your dick"

and I say "No thanks."

We used to work together
    at a furniture store.
She was always asking to suck my dick
in the storeroom and I was always like
"That's very sweet but no thanks"

because she has that creepy vibe
    the kind of vibe
    you don't want
    on your dick

and I see her again
at a terrible afterhours club
in Bloomfield
where all the patrons

are bikers and cokeheads
and she says "I'll suck your dick"
in my ear while I'm ordering a beer

and I say "No thanks"

because I do not want her to suck my dick
even though I like to have my dick sucked

> which must seem incomprehensible
> to someone so intent on sucking.

She's here with a biker who has gray hair
> and a gum-banded goatee
> that hangs to the middle
> of his gray-haired chest

and this time she takes my whole ear
> in her mouth
> and says
"Seriously, I'll suck your dick"

and I say "Stop it"

and she's "What're ya, a faggot?"

and I finish my beer
in an angry swallow and leave.

There are many fine reasons
not to get your dick sucked—
> first and foremost though
is a mean mouth.

## HOLLSOPPLE, PENNSYLVANIA

This town wants god and it wants it now.
Quit getting abortions and arm yourself.
This town wants bumper stickers.
It wants to be a bumper. So it can stick itself.
Jesus is coming to this town. Try Jesus.
He loves bumper stickers and handguns.
He loves America. America loves Jesus.
Love Jesus or die. Tune in to talk radio.
Blame the gays. The gays are always doing it.

Their kissing has angered god.

## AT A GAY BAR IN ALTOONA, PENNSYLVANIA

Did you know the only gay bar in downtown Altoona
is The La Pierre and that The La Pierre translates
from French into English literally as The The Pierre?

Did you know you can be straight and relatively ugly
like myself and still get hit on by a man in fake leather?

My friend Cliff speaks in a swish of a voice
       a sort of rainbow spilling out
       like he's imitating
       the gay best friend
       on a bad TV show
and he says into my answering machine
"You have to help me out again"
       and pauses and says
"I swear this is the last time
but meet me around five at The La Pierre"
       then he makes a dick joke
       followed by another dick joke.

Cliff lives like a horny teenager
and he'd been cheating on Mark
       his partner

with this guy Robert

and because we worked together
       and I was straight
       I was his alibi
his sneaky way out of the house.

So I met him.

I'm not proud.

I am pathetically loyal.

At the bar, Robert
        a fat-fuck
        with dyed
        red hair
        buzzed
        to his scalp
        on the sides
wore dark sunglasses.

Cliff said "Promise you won't leave without me."

I said "Promise" and ordered two beers to help.

Cliff said "I don't love him" about Robert

and I said "Me neither."

I looked at Robert
and that awful hair
and wondered
what a handsome guy
        like Cliff
could find attractive
about such an ugly goof.

I went to the beers
and watched the clock
        like a heart
        about to crack
        and, generally
        moped.

When I looked up
they were gone.

The bar was a shoebox
and they'd sneaked off.

Ten minutes, I thought, and that was it.

      Six minutes later
a man in black leather appeared.

He was a total greaseball
      obviously ripping off the biker
      from the Village People.

He sat down and said
"What's a cute fucker like you
doing in a lousy dump like this?"
      then dramatically
      crunched up
      a piece of ice.

I ordered another beer and said
      "Absolutely nothing."

Then a man dressed like a woman
      sat down beside me.
She (or he) didn't say anything.

The biker dude said "Let me buy you a drink."

I said "Maybe not."

The biker dude was not likeable.

The man dressed like a woman
    had a nice vibe.

The biker dude said "You wanna dance?"

I looked around and opened my ears
    to nothing
    and said
    "No music."

He tilted his leather cap
    adjusted his shades
    and said
"What's it gonna take to get you in bed?"

The obvious answer was:
    umm, a pussy

but I sipped my beer
    and said
    "Nothing."

    He said
"I don't have to do anything
    to get you in bed?"

I said "No."

I said "There's nothing
    you can do
to get me in bed with you."

He adjusted his silly hat
    in an uncomfortable way
    and said

"I don't believe that for a second"
    and flagged down
    the bartender
    with a bill
and ordered two beers.

I said "I can't drink that"

and he said "But why?"

and I said "It might
give you the wrong impression"

and he said "Yeah? What impression is that?"

Two minutes later
my friend Cliff showed up.

He was crying and said
"Oh god, Mark's out there."

I didn't say anything
but of course
Mark was out there.

Where the hell else
is a gay guy
going to look
for his cheating partner
at Happy Hour
in Altoona?

Jesus, I felt bad.

I felt bad for Cliff.

I felt bad for lying to Mark.

I felt bad for thinking Robert
        was such a fat-fuck.

I felt even worse for Robert's awful hairdo
and how it made him look like Satan
        dressed for Christmas.

I felt bad for the biker.

I felt bad for Altoona
        for The La Pierre
            for the entire world.

Love is impossible.

That doesn't begin to include sex.

Cliff quit crying and said
        "Fuck Mark, honestly.
Sometimes he acts like my dad"
and he bought me a beer
and asked me to stick around.

Robert sat down.

The man dressed like a woman
        with the nice vibes
stood up, adjusted his (or her) dress
and headed for the door.

I stood up but not completely.

Robert put his dark sunglasses
        up on his head.

Maybe he didn't look like such a dickwad
       when you could see his eyes.

Maybe his red hair wasn't a punk rock disaster.

I drank the beer.

The biker leaned into me and said
"Not too good to drink with that fag, are you?"

and Cliff said "Back off, bitch, he's straight"

       and the biker said
"And all the inmates are innocent"
and snapped three times in a Z and split.

Cliff said "Don't worry about the biker.
       He's a himbo."

Robert said "What a himbo"

and I said "Yeah, really."

They got up and headed for the corner booth
       like lovers tied up by souls.

I hoped it was worth it for Cliff
       and for Robert too

       and maybe even for Mark
       beautiful Mark
       kind-hearted
       and tolerant Mark
Mark who was probably still out
       in the car, waiting.

Did I say love was impossible?

While Cliff nuzzled Robert in the corner booth
      I started up a conversation
      with a fairly unattractive
          drag queen.

# 3

*America doesn't read poems*
*We barely even share*

# THE GOD IN WALT WHITMAN

Whitman said "In the faces of men and women I see God." I believe that and, because of that, I see God in the face of Walt Whitman, the only poet, ever, who wanted to be praised so he could get down on his knees and worship with the people. When the Civil War broke out, he left his home in Brooklyn, traveled to DC, and volunteered in a hospital for three years. When his little brother, George Washington Whitman, was wounded in battle, Walt immediately rushed into the field to find and care for him. Back at the hospital he spent most of his salary on gifts, candy and tobacco, giving soldiers the love and attention they so desperately needed. That's the God in Whitman and that's why his writing is greater than his writing. He saw the blood and the bones. "Death is nothing here" he wrote in a diary, meaning of course, "Death is everything here." He couldn't leave his tent in the morning to shave without seeing the corpses piled up on stretchers. His refusal to turn away—that's the God in Whitman too. That's why you don't scan his poems for meter. That's why rhyme is useless. That's why I believe it when he said "What a devil thou art, Poverty!" Or, better yet, this: "Stand up for the stupid and crazy." Or, my favorite: "I feel I am of them—I belong to those convicts and prostitutes myself, and henceforth I will not deny them—for how can I deny myself?" It's the God in Whitman that saves us all and it scares the weak and the rich and the powerful. *The Critic* in London didn't see the God in Whitman and the guy who reviewed the first edition of *Leaves of Grass* said: "Whitman is acquainted with art, as a hog is with mathematics." I'm not going to tell you the critic's name. But you know Walt Whitman now or are remembering him again and all of us here know now we have something good to do so let's do it and if that doesn't work—let's do it again.

## NURSE BOB

lives in the house he inherited from his parents
with three men, two of whom he once loved
        and one he loves more every day.

When Bob's father was dying
he said "I always loved you"

and Bob said "I know"

and his father said
"I didn't hate the faggot part
        I was just scared for you"

and Bob said "I know"

and Bob's mom
        at home
        in a hospital bed
said "I never worried about you"

and Bob said "Me neither."

Some men believe in their own greatness
so much that they spend their lives
stomping the hearts of their lovers into dust.

Bob worked part-time and attended
community college to get a nursing degree.

Now he owns his parents' home
and spends his days making patients better
and his nights making loved ones comfortable.

He knows the tragedy of the world is his blessing
        and these are his men:

an unemployed accountant
who can no longer see numbers

an exotic dancer who breathes
with an oxygen tube up his nose

and the kitchen manager
from The Haddington Hotel
on Kutcher Boulevard.

The nights are filled
with long wet coughs
and enough laughter
to distance the grave.

Bob cried every day
when he was 13
because his best friend
asked for a kiss
      then
         as Bob leaned in
punched him in the nose.

If you believe in time
the years will change everything.

Bob forgives everyone
even those who do not ask.

Each night he comes home to
      an accountant
      a dancer
      and a manager.

Two of these men will see
two of these men to the light.

# IN MEMORY OF ARTHUR RIMBAUD

A teenager shoots out my neighbor's window
with a shotgun then another neighbor's window
then he shoots a dumpster outside Walmart.

The cops don't catch the kid
and my neighbors are furious
and the people in town are furious

but I am not furious.

The teenager has cost us some glass
and some wood and a gallon of paint
or less and a few hours of labor

which seems a fair price
to have teenagers in the world
who shoot but not to kill

so I consider this a gift.

I too was a small-time vandal
a destroyer of the neighborhood
out of boredom and desire

so that trees chopped themselves
when I walked by and mailboxes
spit letters and toppled in my presence

and now I work overtime without pay.

From the creek running through my backyard
the teenager shoots the side window
of my apartment while I am at work.

The screen rips up and the window cracks
and some pellets stick in the glass
and some pellets come through

but nothing is unrepairable.

I mean to call the landlord but it's dark
and he beds down in the early evening
and I work the early shift the next morning

unloading a truck then switching
to a tie to appear managerial
as I stay late to cover a shift

for a co-worker with a sick kid.

I do something like this for a couple days
working and eating and walking in the woods
until one night I feel a bite on my neck

and flick on the light and a dozen mosquitoes
have come in through the holes in the glass
and their wings are like beams of light

and their legs skinny like tiny old alcoholic men

wobbling off barstools to face their wives.
I sleep the night in the bathtub
a blanket pulled up over my head.

Thank you, teenager, for reminding me to itch.

## THE ROAD TO GOD

Thoreau, who believed in ponds
    who hated slavery
    who hated war

who cared for the writings
    of Walt Whitman

while not really caring
for Walt Whitman, the egomaniac
    the starstruck Whitman
    the needy Whitman
    Whitman
    who could not
    have been
    alone on a pond
who maybe loved America
    too much
but who could, nonetheless,
    write like an angel

    Thoreau who
when wondering about
the spirituality that illuminates
so many of the passages
in *Leaves of Grass*
asked Whitman if he'd ever read
    the *Bhagavad Gita*
    or any of the other
    spiritual writings
    of India

and Whitman said:
"No, tell me more."

## A REDNECK BAR IN THE HEART OF PENNSYLVANIA
*—for Todd Cirelli*

We shot pool with some strangers
at a dive called The Boiler Room.

Nobody looked like us, talked like us
drank or even chewed like us.

I sipped a warm draft Blatz
and kicked my legs over the stool.

Todd chalked his stick
and started knocking in balls.

The bank shot was lucky.
The jump shot was arrogant.

Over in the corner, three guys in flannels,
bushy beards and camo hunting caps

munched hot wings and waited
for their chance at the eight ball.

The $4^{th}$ guy, chewing a chicken bone
like a weed, followed Todd around

saying "We don't shoot that hard stick
if ya know what I'm saying."

I knew what he was saying.
Todd, on his $10^{th}$ beer, didn't.

He put the stick behind his back
in a hotshot move and sank another ball.

God bless Todd. He's so good-looking
that men often want to destroy his face.

The mean guy said "I don't know if that's
a good shot if you're not from these parts."

Todd cranked in another ball, slugged
some beer and said "Yeah right, hard stick."

The three boys in the corner booth looked up
to see what the ruckus was about then wiped

their greasy barbecue mouths with paper napkins
like a synchronized team of backwoods assassins.

I sat there and drank my crummy beer
wondering if, perhaps, I could outrun

a pickup truck while somehow
managing to find a better bar.

## MISERABLE

Inside the Pipe Room, the hometown dive
where all the locals play pool and guzzle beer

a cute short blonde woman, seven years my senior
who used to be a sergeant in the U.S. Army

says "He doesn't respect me"
meaning her fiancé, a professor at Saint Francis.

He's 20 years her senior and makes a lot of money.
He wants to give her a good life

with stuff and credit cards that don't have limits.
She's miserable with all of it.

She's supported herself since she was 17
and she doesn't need his help

(though she's drinking on his MasterCard)
and besides, he reads too many books.

"I read a lot of books" I say
and she says "That's different."

She's right but I don't know why.
I buy her a vodka.

The smoke here is unbelievable.
The jukebox is too loud.

Somehow, I've convinced myself
that I'm getting laid.

She puts the next round
and the next on his MasterCard.

She kisses me full on the mouth.
Then it's last call.

She says "He crushes my dreams with his cynicism."
Sometimes I crush my own dreams with my own cynicism.

Outside, there is rain and whatever else we have at home.

## TEMPORARY

I go back to a temp place
because I'm still laid off

and the woman says
"You don't have a license?"

and I say "I have a license.
I just don't have it with me"

and she says "Who comes to an interview
without identification?"

and I say "I thought it'd be less formal"
which it was last week

when I'd written my Social Security number
on a five-line application.

My car has three cylinders and brakes that grind
and hasn't been insured in six months.

I thought I'd throw some boxes today
or paint houses or snap together blinds

on an assembly line
and get a check without taxes taken out

and the secretary would cash it
just like last week

when I showed up without ID
and spent a day on a moving crew

rolling up fancy carpets in the South Hills
until my knees burned

until I collected my check
$75, all take-home

and I said "No taxes?"
and a guy in an unknotted tie

sputtered over his lips and said
"You're technically a subcontractor"

which meant, technically, nothing
so I autographed the check

and came back the next day
and the next and the next

until I'd paid the phone bill
and bought two pounds of chipped ham

then I spent two days sending out resumes
and one day writing poems

then one night drunk
and now I'm back here

still without ID
and the man with the unknotted tie

is somewhere else
maybe somewhere more permanent

replaced by a woman
in a pit-stained dress

who looks like she lives on
chili fries and made-to-order subs

who smells like ketchup
and peppermint Certs

who says "No ID, no work"
and takes a slug of diet A&W

and I say "Seriously?"
but nice, like I want to snap

my bones for money
until I'm kneeless and crooked

and, look, these are my best khakis.
These are my only good pair of pants.

# HIGHWAY CRIMES

He had a studio apartment in Greensburg
and there was a map of Southwestern
Pennsylvania taped to his living room wall.
Little red thumbtacks marked convenience
stores with access to main roads or highways.
I said "Convenience stores, you're kidding?"
I knew he had balls but this was a bad joke.
With a beer in one hand and a smoke in the other
he pointed at the map and said "I've never
been more serious about anything in my life."
He was a welder without credentials and
he was sick of the lousy pay. But who wasn't?
I was driving truck then and I knew this guy
in Florida and he wanted me to run all this
marijuana from South Bay up to Michigan.
He named a number and it was more than
I'd make in a year. I looked back at my friend
with his ridiculous map of convenience stores.
The map looked like it'd been folded fifty
times so some of the creases looked like roads
and some of the roads disappeared into creases.
My friend said "At least three hundred a store."
Three hundred a store, right. For five years in jail.
Don't talk to me about guns. I don't wear disguises.
All those thumbtacks. All those pushed-in dreams.

## LEGALIZE EVERYTHING

I wish this—all of it—was legal
    because
I always worry that
doing illegal things
will put me in jail
but not enough
to stop doing
illegal things
which are
more fun
and help more
than most
of the legality
in my life—example:
    minimum wage.

## DENTAL INSURANCE

Every time I drink a Coke
    I lick my teeth
          and think about

going bankrupt.

## THE DENTIST SAYS

"You really haven't been here in 13 years?"

"Uh huh" I say with his fingers in my mouth
        meaning: who can afford this shit?

"Not a single cavity" he says.

My last job wanted $80 a month
        just for teeth
               not eyes or brain
               or anything
               below the jaw.

The dentist says "Unbelievable."

But believable, I think.

I floss. I brush. I rinse and spit.

America depends on those of us
with good teeth to do without
so those of us with money
and all kinds of teeth
        may do with.

Rise up, brothers and sisters.
        I go down smiling.

## OUTSIDE THE LOBSTER TRAP BAR

in Johnstown, Pennsylvania
a man takes a hard right
to the face then falls
then gets kicked in the gut.

From the gravel lot
he looks up at his tormentor
      and
with a bloody mouth
      says

"I'm a man, and you know it!"

## JOHNSTOWN, PENNSYLVANIA

The chief of police
tasered his son
at Thanksgiving dinner.

## SHE HAS HER PERIOD

and the bouncer
who makes the schedule
won't let her work
if he finds out
    which he shouldn't
but he's the kind of creep
who looks at your belly
and says "Holding water, babe?"
    which is fucking gross
which is fucking ridiculous

which is what you take
to not give allergy shots
to screaming children
for $10 an hour.

This isn't even a real strip joint.
Girls have to wear bottoms
because the bar serves booze
and you can't serve booze
and show your pussy
    which doesn't make sense
    except it does
when you see how drunk
the customers get—
one goof tried to kiss her clit
right through her bikini
    just puckered up
    and planted one
    right on her pubes.

Last year she worked at Walmart
    the only white chick cashier

and half the black chicks
who were 17 and 19 and 20
    all had babies
and the one Asian chick
was like 65 fucking years old.

Now she drinks warm water from the microwave
    and walks around the apartment.

She turns on the TV and watches
an episode of *Deadwood*
which is pretty good—
cowboy types saying the fuck word
like people do in real life
and this doctor who's addicted to morphine
and this bartender who's almost a motherfucker
and Wild Bill Hycock who is mostly a drunk
and Calamity Jane who is clearly a lesbian
    whether she knows it or not
and this other chick with cerebral palsy
who sweeps up at the whorehouse
and everyone is real sweet to
and no one wants to fuck.

Sweet men not wanting to fuck you
    always sounds good
    but really, no.

She's been going to the employment center
    taking the prep course for her GED
    but it's like retard stuff
        stuff they taught in 8$^{th}$ grade

and she doesn't want a degree
    anymore than she wants

        to marry her boyfriend
        who is a mechanic at Pep Boys
        and makes good money
        and pays for the HBO
which is the station
playing *Deadwood*.

See how they trap you.
See how they get you to do
when what you want most
        is to not.

The rent isn't due for another 10 days
and she has 900 bucks in a plastic baggie
stuffed in the bottom of a maxipad box
her mom dropped off five years ago
because they were on sale.
        Who uses maxipads?
        It's like wearing a diaper.

She goes to the kitchen and dials Fatso
        the bouncer who weighs 150 pounds
        and calls off for tonight
        and tomorrow night too.

Then she makes some microwave popcorn
        and adds extra butter and salt
        which is what she likes to do
when she has her period and feels like a grump.

# THE BOUNCER BOUNCES

The bartenders bartend
and the waitresses wait

and the dude coming later
will clean the toilets

and sweep the floors
and the cook, of course, cooks

though sometimes the bartenders
wait tables and the waitresses bartend

and the cook will barback
and the dude coming later

to clean the toilets
will smoke cigarettes in the alley.

But the bouncer bounces.
It is written as law.

Should you be so inclined
to have your head placed

in the vice of his arm
speak up.

## AT A STRIP BAR IN THE MIDDLE OF PENNSYLVANIA

She moves my beer bottle out of reach
and says "I have a clumsy ass."

Spread across the bar she scissor-kicks
grabs on to her ankles and cradles her tit.

Some Japanese writing is tattooed
a few inches to the left of her g-string.

I try to figure out the design
while she makes sexy stripper faces.

She points at the ink and says "Mother first."
"As in?" I say.

She crawls back on to the dance floor.
"As in" she says "I have kids at home."

I take a swig off my beer
and stop to applaud the moment.

She leans in to me with a smile
her tits pushed together like a basket.

I give her one dollar for the performance
another dollar for the kids at home.

She thanks me with a kiss on the cheek
then pets my head like a small poodle.

# SHAKESPEARE ON THE DOWN LOW

I work 14 days straight at the furniture store
        60 hours a week
        none of it paid overtime
        because I'm the manager

        then I make sure
        the next day, payday
        is covered

which, miraculously, it is—

no one has the flu
or a sick kid
or a migraine
or their period

so I buy some beer and drive west
to Homewood to get drugs
from a guy named D'Money
        the oldest student
        currently enrolled
        in general studies
at the Community College of Allegheny County.

The last time I was here
        he was studying
        seriously and unsuccessfully
        hoping to finish
        his two-year degree
        and transfer
        to a university.

In movies, drug dealers are always smart
        reading scales like scientists
but D'Money is mostly muscle
        who knew someone
        who knew someone
        who probably killed someone
        who knew someone else
        who had a cousin
        who liked D'Money

and D'Money stepped up
and has been hustling for 40 years.

Last visit I offered to help with his math
        which was addition and subtraction
        but with large numbers
        like 3456 + 1200 = X
        and maybe the X makes it Algebra
or not, I don't know.

The place is fucking packed
and D'Money looks high
though he claims to not get high
but how can you not get high
when your business is fucking people up?

A group stands in a circle
        smoking PCP
which really sounds horrible
and really smells horrible
and other people are getting stoned
and other-other people are too stoned
        to be getting stoned anymore.

D'Money says "White people are smart"

and I say "Not really"

which is as true
as anything else.

The TV is on and someone
        for unknown reasons
says something about Shakespeare

and D'Money says "Shakespeare—
he a reader or a writer?"

like these things are mutually exclusive
        two separate categories
        like you can write
        without devouring books

and before anyone can laugh
        because, really
we're all afraid to laugh

someone says "I think Shakespeare was a reader"

and everyone goes back to being stoned
        or waiting to buy whatever it is
        that will make us stoned

and D'Money looks up from his pile of loot
        and says "Yeah, so what the fuck he read?"

# DRINKING AND DRUGGING

He said "Do you ever think that if you quit drinking and doing drugs and applied yourself, you'd be a lot better off in the world?"

I considered the question seriously because it was something I'd asked myself years before after graduating with a 4.0 GPA in a master's program then, after applying for 50 jobs, went to work as a industrial parts delivery man. It was a question I'd asked myself when I was a janitor and when I was a box loader and when I was a huffer for a moving company. It was a question I'd asked myself when I wrote my 23rd novel and sent it to an agent who said he couldn't sell it to a big New York house because it wasn't set in New York and none of the women cared about shoes. Basically, honestly, I wake up every morning and ask myself: what the fuck are you doing wrong? because I want to do it right but, as far as I can tell—speaking as someone who doesn't watch TV or have many friends or, basically, sleep—drinking and drugging for recreation and the occasional answer to anxiety are the least of it

though I wished for drink and drugs in enormous quantities when I attended the company annual meeting in Atlanta and the CEO, a former Walmart higher-up who'd been mentored by Sam Walton, showed up on a horse, on a real-live fucking horse in the ballroom of a 4-fucking-star hotel, and took the stage with a microphone and proceeded to shout down individual employees over various infractions, from buying garbage cans to using too much tissue paper, until half the audience was in tears and the country music act scheduled to perform later in the evening stepped out of the audience and presented the CEO with a signed guitar.

What was the question?

Do I ever think that if I quit drinking and doing drugs and applied myself, I'd be a lot better off in the world?

No.

## THEY CLOSE THE STORE

The district manager calls to say
the store is going to be closed this summer

and I say "But we're doing great"
and go digging for my reports

and she says "That's true"
so I quit digging for my reports

thinking she's reconsidered
because she agrees we're doing great

but she says
"These are always odd decisions"

and I say
"So we're not closing?"

and she says
"No, you're definitely closing"

and I say
"But we're doing great"

and she says
"Don't tell anyone else

that we're closing the store"
and hangs up.

Last month she gave me
an average review

because I'd written
above-average reviews

for all my employees
when the unspoken goal

had been to give everyone
below-average reviews

especially to those
who were exceptional.

So I go out
and tell everyone

both exceptional
and unexceptional

that the store is being closed
in the next month or so

and after a few moments of panic
and a few moments of sadness

and a few moments of anger
and a few moments of regrouping

someone asks
"Can we steal shit?"

and I say "Yes."

# DREAM THE ILLITERATE DREAM OR DON'T DREAM AT ALL

She says "What are you going to do
now that you don't have a job?"

and I say "Collect unemployment
and write novels about Pittsburgh."

and she says "That's stupid."
She says "You should write porn."

# AUTOBIOGRAPHY OF A TIGHT VAGINA

Is it wrong
that I think
a small penis
is a plus?

# THE STANDARD REJECTION LETTER

I send a query letter and some short stories
and the New York publisher says "Sure!"

so I send along my novel.
My novel is 275 pages long.

I feel like should say something
more than that in my cover letter.

Remember me? Here's my book:
I'm the next Charles Dickens:

I'm great, I've been rejected
300 times by *The New Yorker*!

Writing queries and correspondences
makes me feel like a used car salesman

and I write maybe exclusively
not to feel like a used car salesman

so I don't say anything
and lick the envelope shut.

I think: done!
though I don't know what done means

except that I immediately start
writing another book.

I'm old enough to understand
this all ends

not with fame or money
or even a job teaching college

but with me writing another book
and another book after that.

A year later my novel comes back
dog-eared and missing pages.

No one where I live writes books
and no one read books when I was growing up

and when I am around other writers
they generally treat me like a trained gorilla.

The standard rejection letter
always starts: we regret to inform you …

I regret to inform myself
something similar every day

then upon sitting down to write
I open up and rejoice.

# CARPENTER

For the last 15 years I've searched
the want ads like a dictionary
in reverse, a dictionary filled
with incomprehensible definitions

and here, today, the word *carpenter*
the letters lined up like a new house
        with an open door

but I've been to college
and fallen in love with language

and gone back to college

and gone back to college again

and still I lack good work.

My father was an electrician
with an 8th-grade education
who believed degrees
would make his children rich

and I am the opposite of rich

though I love wood and the shape of things
        the way trees fall and grow back.

My grandfather's first job was in a lumberyard
and he talked about the smell of sawdust
        for the next 80 years.

Here's the house I built in my mind.

I'd like to sell it to your mind but maybe
you need a new kitchen or a better roof.

Carpenter. How in all my years of college
      I never learned to pound a nail.

## TODAY I ALMOST CALLED McDONALD'S

to see about their manager training program
Hamburger U as it was called in the want ads

then I came to my senses, called the bank
and put a stop on the check that was supposed

to be for my electric bill because who needs light
during the summer and it's July now, bright

until late in the day and, besides, I worked
for Burger King before and I hated

getting burned by fry grease and the manager
kept pinching my ass and being snide

so I settled back on the couch for a snooze
then sent out two resumes for jobs

I'm not qualified for or I'm overqualified for
meaning I went to school forever

but never acquired a marketable skill
because I thought attending school made me marketable

but instead I got a job as a janitor then a daycare worker
then I drove truck and I once sold steroids to muscleheads

which makes my resume impossible to explain
to the district manager of a Bed Bath & Beyond

like I needed to do last month when he looked at me
and said "Why, exactly, would I want to hire you?"

and I didn't have an answer for him, just like
I don't know why I applied for those jobs today

because I really wouldn't want to manage
a hardware store or a lumber yard, considering

I never learned how to drive a nail in college
where they wanted me to read Focault

which made me want to put my head in the oven
or smoke a tailpipe in a locked garage

so I'm broke and not thinking rationally
and I wish someone paid for that

because I'm great at it, dreaming I mean
but the bills keep piling up

and the lady from the student loan company
says "You really need to get straight with us"

which was the problem to begin with
believing an education would get me straight

when all it did was confuse everything
and make me not want to work at anything

but writing poems in my little apartment
and, besides, what kind of company

lends money to a guy who believes
he can make a living writing poems in America.

America doesn't read poems.
We barely even share.

## PEOPLE WHO TALK ABOUT BEING BROKE

almost never are:

see how they fly across the country
like planes are little ponies
you drop quarters into and ride

and how they manage vacations
more distant than the corner bar.

People who are broke
never talk about being broke.

They're ashamed.

# THE INTERVIEW

For I am overeducated and overqualified.
For I am undereducated and underqualified.
For I try to look thoughtful and think between questions.
For my answers to the questions are too slow.
For the powerless never speak fast enough for the powerful.
For the woman asking questions looks disgusted.
For the man asking questions looks angry.
For the woman asking questions wears a better suit.
For the man asking questions wears a hardhat.
For it is very hot in this room.
For no one has offered me any water.
For my mouth is as dry as an old shoe in the sun.
For please provide an example of a poor employee
and how you handled said employee in crisis.
For I am asked questions about my degrees.
For I quote from Time magazine
about the importance of a liberal arts education.
For the interviewer looks confused.
For there are many interviewers and much confusion.
For shouldn't I just be a writer then?
For aren't writers usually rich and publish books?
For I am lying again, when I said I would not lie.
For I am drenched in sweat and have to cough.
For, exactly, why should I be hired?
For I am a people person and I love people
and am a self-starter who loves to start.
For I am curious about the air conditioner in here.
For my lips taste like sweat dripping from my forehead.
For you've answered all my questions, thanks.
For let's shake with my wet right hand, thanks.
For I hope to hear from you, thanks.
For I can show myself the door.

## FAT

Jen says "I'm dying"

and I say "Not before you buy me a beer."

Franny keeps fixing his long hair
so we pretend not to notice he's going bald.

Today is Thursday, which is almost Friday.
Friday still means something, despite misfortune.

I have interviewed for 10 jobs in 12 days
        two of which
        pay more than
        poverty wages.

The bar here has stools made from elephant legs
        and a stuffed lion
        behind glass
        looking less than fierce.

Jen thinks I should fly her to Vegas
        and make her my wife.

"Just for the night" she says.

"Probably not" I say.

I have nine dollars.

Franny is angry that his girlfriend
        is so fucking fat.
She's not fat, exactly, just bigger
        than when they met.

Franny says "Like 60 pounds bigger."

Jen says "Am I fat?"

and I say "No, you're sexy."

Fat is me in the mirror and how
I'm almost shaped like a beer bottle.

Franny says "It's not healthy to be that heavy"
    but what he means is:
    my old skinny girlfriend
    could see me
    with my new fat girlfriend
    and I'll look like a fucking loser.

Franny should quit being so shallow.

Then he should buy me a beer.

Then someone should hire me.

Jen stands up then falls down.

Franny points at me and says
"You could lose a little weight too, fatso."

He's right: I look bad in a suit.

Jen climbs back from the floor, angry.

She says "Don't call him that"

and I say "Thank you, Jen."

We've been coming to this bar a lot lately.

The elephant legs are pretty uncomfortable
       but the drinks are cheap.

Jen works six days a week as a waitress.

I have two degrees and a plethora
       of experiences.

       Everyone knows
       Franny's fat girlfriend
       still fucks
       her old ex-boyfriend
who has more money than Franny
and is at least as ugly, maybe worse.

I'm available to start immediately.

# FRANK

punches me in the mouth
and I step back and spit blood.

Frank is small and mean
and fights often but not well.

Last week we unloaded trucks together
and this week I drove a truck
      that Frank unloaded.

Frank cannot drive a truck
because he does not have
the proper credentials
but Frank says he can
drive a truck and would like to.

He swings again and I move
      but not fast enough
and he hits me in the neck.

I can either punch Frank back
or walk away but walking away
does not mean I am safe
      from another punch.

This is my whole life.

## THE WRONG SIDE OF THE BED

Kimberly drops the kids at daycare
then drives straight to the office

then signs in and starts typing an abstract
then sneaks away for coffee and a cigarette

then sneaks back in
like she wasn't smoking and caffeinating.

She thinks about her sons all day
the redhead and the brunette

how they hold hands as they walk through the world
so the day is not a complete loss

though she'd like to not punch in data
for a bunch of research doctors

who make their employees sneak
who would never sneak themselves

who guzzle coffee and gossip
about the newest yoga place

or the newest hot yoga place
or the newest aerial yoga place

or the hottest vegetarian restaurant.
Why do rich people not eat meat?

What the fuck is aerial yoga?
Who has time for vegetables and exercise?

Kimberly will be 28 in March.
She's never not had a job

which is half a lie, maybe less
because she's worked since she was 12

first at her grandma's catering business
then in restaurants

then in bars, mostly dives
then in a university lab

while she was going to school
for biology and pre-med

biology, which she loved
especially cells

especially how her science teacher
back in high school

called them the building blocks of life
though she would still be in college

if she hadn't built her second kid's life
with a bartender named Roman

who is in Greece right now
30 years old and still wearing a backpack.

The first father, who she loved
who she misses desperately

whose memory she tried to fuck away
with Roman the backpacker

died at 25 from brain cancer
never smoked, barely drank

the only man ever
who could dance a tango

and make it look badass
not like he was looking to get laid

but like he was about to stomp
a hole in the world's heart

so people like her
could step through untouched.

She has the two boys who are hers alone
but she is alone, despite that

because her parents are useless
one drinking, one playing slots

and the days are endlessly cold
and sometimes she weeps in traffic.

At night Kimberly sleeps
on the wrong side of the bed

to be close to the memory
of her dead husband

and weekends she watches
terrible movies just to see couples dance.

The world will never be the same,
even if it is, because love is like that.

Love is always like that.
How else would we survive?

## THE BEER FACTORY

I got an interview at the Beer Factory. The manager was made of glass and his office was a refrigerator. He had a liver that poked through his cotton shirt and a gut the size of a half barrel.

He said "How much do you drink?"

I said "A lot."

Then I showed him.

Six months later and I'm completely bored. Everyone stinks like booze and pukes a lot. The woman next to me wears too much lipstick and the man at the front desk keeps throwing darts at my chest and hitting my balls with a pool cue. For lunch I have sex with my boss but she keeps forgetting my name and I'm always too drunk to come.

Yesterday, driving home from work, I ran over my toe.

## THE POEM FACTORY

I got an interview at the Poem Factory. It cost me 25 dollars to get in the door. The editor had been educated at Harvard but hated Harvard and now hired poets from around the world to work with language.

He said "Why should I hire you?"

I said "I'm a poem person. I like poems."

He said "Have you ever worked with poems before?"

I said "I've worked with poems in books and magazines and in the classroom."

He said "How much do you expect to make working in the Poem Factory?"

I said "Almost nothing."

He looked at me.

I said "Nothing?"

I said "I'd be happy to pay an additional contest fee of up to 25 dollars."

Well, he hired me. I work in the basement and I have no idea what I'm doing but neither does anyone else down here. The women in the blurb department speak the loudest while the rest of us wear earplugs and blindfolds and have specific instructions to reward only the best and brightest, the nonsensical language makers, the political sloganeers.

"To heaven we all go," said William Blake.

My tongue barely works and I'm verging on bankrupt but what's that even mean after 40 hours per week of literature and fine art?

When I think back to my interview, I am so filled with light I burn pages.

# THE OLD DRUNKEN IMMORTALS

*Must be heaven's immortals in a drunken frenzy*
*grabbing cloud and grinding it into white dust*
                                              *—Li Po*

On my lunch break I sneak off
        to read some Li Po poems.

An hour later I have everyone talking
about grabbing cloud and grinding dust.

Nobody cares what it means
        they just like the sound
        especially drunken frenzy
        a poetry better than
        carrying furniture
        or mandatory overtime.

Eventually one guys asks "Who wrote that?"

and I say "Li Po, the great Chinese poet"

and he says "Ah yes, dank you berry much"
in the worst Chinese accent this side
        of a 1930s Charlie Chan movie
and starts to bow like a humble servant.

Pretty soon everyone bows
        like humble servants
        because we are
        humble servants

                and I bow
                the deepest

and someone asks "Li Po dead?"
and I say "Like 1200 years ago"

and someone else asks "Did Li Po drink?"

and I say "Li Po was an immortal drunk.
He couldn't keep a job because he was drunk"

only now I'm carrying
a wall-length mirror
balanced on my hip

while telling the story of Li Po
      how he was smashed on wine
      high in the mountains
      and saw the reflection
      of the moon shimmering
      on the surface of a lake
      and how he decided
      he would make love
      to her, the moon,
      so he wrote a note
            left it by a rock
            with his wine bottle
      then dove 100 feet
      like some strange bird
            and drowned

which is more or less true
or more or less not true

because another book says
he fell from a small boat
while trying to embrace the moon

                not as interesting
                as diving and fucking
but such is the myth of Li Po:

                you tell it
how you need to tell it.

If you are broke, Li Po is your poet.
If you are kind, Li Po is your poet.
If your hands are covered in blisters
and your legs cramp when you work
                if you are so buried in debt
                the sky looks like a bill
                Li Po is your poet.

                        So celebrate.

I move to the truck with a mirror on my hip
like I have wings, like an angel, like I can fly

like I don't give a fuck, like a drunk Li Po

whose story I tell with wine, with height
                with danger and a horrible splash

and the mirror slips

and the mirror falls

and the mirror shatters

until I stand over my reflection
in hundreds of ugly pieces

and really: what the fuck is poetry?

The books I've read
are nowhere near
the number of hours
I've worked.

    One terrible co-worker says
"You're gonna get fucking docked"
and wipes his forehead with his t-shirt

and another terrible co-worker says
"You're gonna get fired"
        and points his finger
        like a pistol
        and shoots the bullet
        with his mouth.

The glass is on the street and I need a broom—

        such is my own myth
            one of ineptitude
            sobriety
            and clumsy work.

Later my boss shows up and says
"The truck is going to California.
They probably won't remember
        their stupid fucking mirror"

meaning I'll pay for it if they do
        and later
a guy who will soon leave this job
        to start dealing hard drugs
        says "What's that mean?
        The thing about the immortals
        in a drunken frenzy,

             the clouds
             and the white dust?"

and I tell him it's about snow
             it's about Li Po
             in the courtyard during winter
             it's about noticing the details
             the world walks over
             before they're stomped
                     to mud

             and he says "Shit,
             I thought it was about cocaine."

## EVERYBODY DREAMS OF WIELDING A RIVET GUN FOR TWENTY BUCKS AN HOUR
   *—for Ben Hamper*

I have a friend in Detroit who married a woman
whose dad is a higher-up in the automotive industry

and the dad got my friend a good gig as a negotiator
      going between union and management

and my friend calls to say Ford is hiring (again)
      1200 people, total
      400 in the first wave.

My name is on the master list in Dearborn
at the Employment Office
      down around number 3000
      so I'm in for jackshit

but my pal talks to his wife who talks to her dad
and the dad and my pal both talk to the union rep
      a supposedly good guy
      who tells lies
      to everyone equally
and this guy makes some promises (again).

My pal says "What do you think?"

and I say "Great"

because even though I know
the assembly line would be tough
      I've done tough already
three or four or ten times
      moving company

    truck driver
    retail manager
    UPS
    bouncer, etc.
(so has everyone, I'm not bragging)
but at least the assembly line pays
and offers benefits and paid vacation.

Hazy, coming off twelve hours on the graveyard shift
but with the white cloud of hope floating me up
    I hit the PA Turnpike
and drive 320 miles in less than 5 hours.

By noon, I sit in the waiting room of a small office
in an industrial plaza, filling out an application
    my fifth in three years for Ford
printing all my jobs in neat letters
    in tiny columns
    even though my job-jumping
    makes me look manic
    like a disloyal employee
because I constantly and desperately leave jobs
    for other jobs
    that pay better
    but not remotely enough

plus I have all this education
    unrelated to anything
    and on the application
    where it asks
    how many grades
    I've completed
    I write 18
      meaning:
12 years of public school

4 years of college
and 2 years of graduate school
when what they want to know is:

    can you read?

which I can and do
but would not
on the assembly line
if you would hire me, sir.

## FROM THE COUNTRY TO SMACK

Two deer drink from a creek while I watch
and listen to the warble of running water.

The ranger drives his Jeep slowly
and I lean hard against a tree.

My unemployment is in its sixth and final month
and the rent comes due on my apartment in days.

I understand that I'm failing miserably
and that writing about it won't help.

When I stand up and grab my sack
one of the deer startles and makes the brush.

The other cranes his neck then goes back
to the water, his tongue against a rock.

A couple miles of trail to my old car
three miles to what is left of my home.

When I said writing wouldn't help
I meant money.

When I said I was failing miserably
I meant money.

When I hit the city at midnight
with what was left of my money

and touch down with some dope
I mean that is all.

Acknowledgements:

Thanks to the editors of the following magazines for publishing some of these poems (usually in different forms and sometimes with different titles):

Chiron Review, 5AM, Nerve Cowboy, No Tell Motel, Pittsburgh City Paper, Poetry Motel, Rattle, and Word Riot.

Some of these poems also appeared in the chapbook Allen Ginsberg Comes to Pittsburgh, published by Platonic 3Way Press. One of these poems appeared in the limited-edition collection, You Won't See Me Drinking with Scott Silsbe This Thursday Night, That's for Sure, published exclusively in France.

"Empty" appeared on the How a Poem Happens website, along with a short author interview. Thanks Brian Brodeur.

Thanks to Mike Baron for all he does with White Gorilla Press. You're the goods, Mike. Publishing books has never been this much fun.

Thanks to Jakiela, for everything, always.

Made in the USA
Middletown, DE
12 August 2016